Author: **Katie Middleton**

Illustrator: **JJ Sun**

Thinking Outside the Square

ISBN:
978-1-7773626-0-7 Hardcover
978-1-7773626-1-4 Ebook
978-1-7773626-2-1 Softcover

Cover design and illustrations: JJ Sun

Acknowledgement:

We acknowledge that we live, write and play
on the traditional, ancestral and unceded territory
of the Coast Salish peoples–
Sḵwx̱wú7mesh (Squamish),
Stó:lō and Səl̓ílwətaʔ/Selilwitulh (Tsleil-Waututh)
and xʷməθkʷəy̓əm (Musqueam) Nations.

We would like to dedicate this book
to the more than 150,000 indigenous children
and their families across Canada
who endured the residential school system.

Hi. Let me introduce myself!
You may know me as a square,
but my full name is **Polygon**
Qua-dri-la-te-ral...
phew! That's why everyone
just calls me **Poly**.

I come from a long line of Quadrilaterals - that is - We all have 4 sides.

I'm a square, equal in every way. My mom is a rhombus and my dad is a rectangle.

My aunt did some research into our family tree, and we may have a kite on my grandpa's side!

MY FAMILY TREE

Poly - baby square

Baby isosceles trapezoid

Mom rhombus

Dad rectangle

Aunt trapezoid

Grandma parallelogram

Grandpa quadrilateral

kite

Sorry if I talk too much.

Sometimes I get a bit

lonely.

You see,

my family and I moved

to this town not too long

ago, and **fitting in**

has been really hard.

2D TOWN
WELCOME
MOVING CO.

My second week here, I met two circles named

Cara and Calvin.

They seemed keen on

being **friends**, but...

I had a really hard time **rolling** with them because of my 4 **corners**.

I even accidentally **poked** Cara ...

... That was the end of that.

Z z z
That night Poly went to bed, sad that he hadn't made friends yet.

He dreamt about Cara and Calvin and what it would take to become a circle.

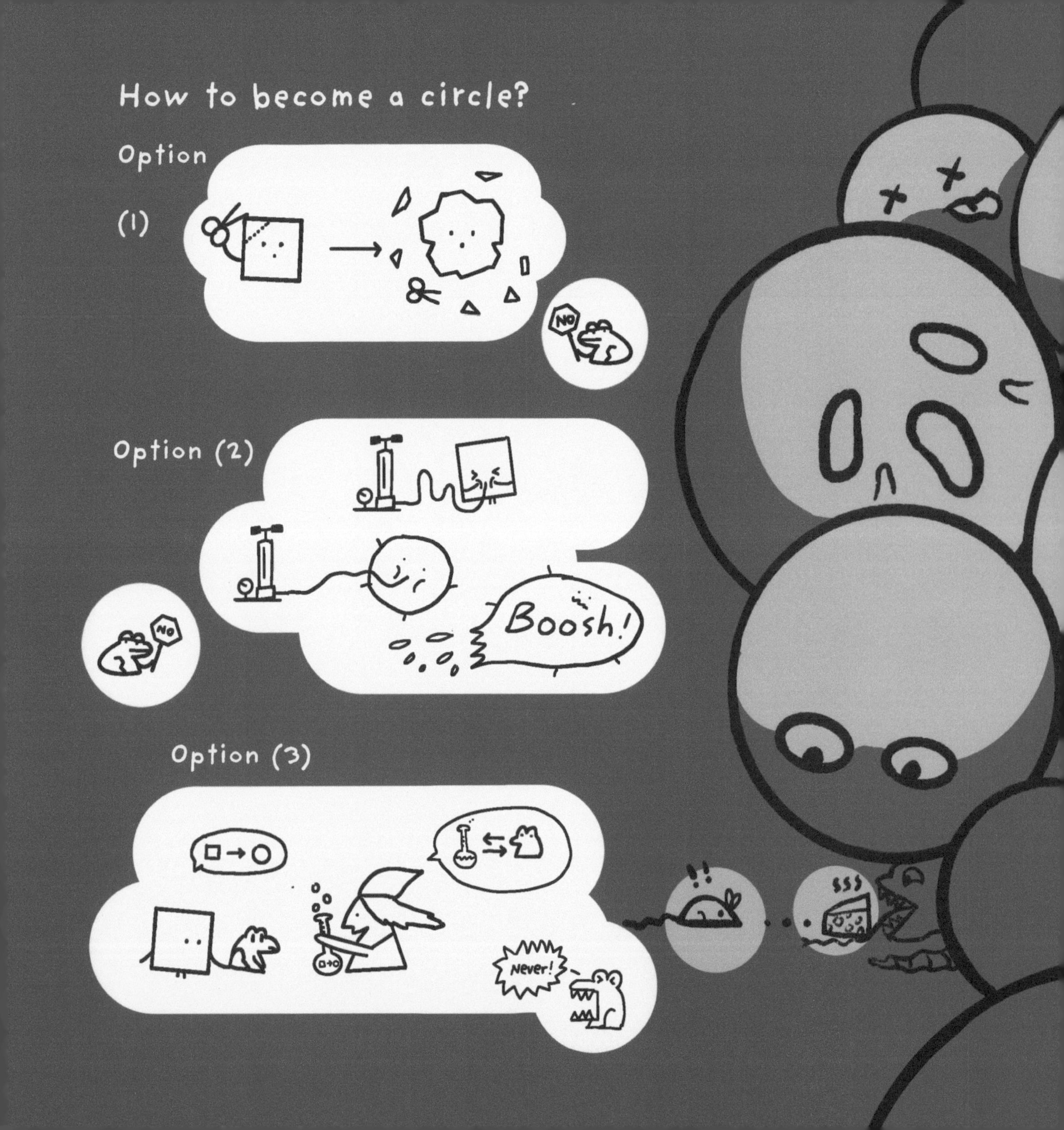

How to become a circle?

Option (1)

NO

Option (2)

Boosh!

NO

Option (3)

Never!

Poly awoke in a cold sweat, terrified at the thought of his dreams, but very glad to be awake now.

He rushed over to the mirror.

Phew, all my corners are still there!

Do squares really try to fit in by changing their shape?

Poly followed his mom's advice for a great morning routine. Self-care really did help him feel a whole lot better!

Now feeling more relaxed, Poly decided to go out for a walk.

Walking down the sidewalk, Poly was still reflecting on his dreams. Looking out into nature, he noticed that every tree, every bush, every rock, every bird had their own unique shape and place.

There must be a place for me too!

Distracted by his thoughts, Poly tripped on a rock.

CRASH!

BANG!

A friendly hand reached
out to help Poly up.

Thanks very much.
Hmm you look
familiar...

My name is Kenneth Kite,
but you can call me uncle Ken.
I'm part of the **Quadrilateral**
family but left at a young age to
travel and pursue my curiosity
about the world around me.

I'm Poly. I think
I've seen you in
family pictures. It's
great to finally
meet you...uh...uncle
Ken. Fitting in has
been hard.

It's great to meet you as well
Poly. I understand how you feel.
It can certainly be difficult
moving to a new town.

Here, come follow me...

Thanks uncle Ken! I can see you've been on some grand adventures!

I have learned a lot through my travels and observing different shapes around the world. **Knowledge is important** Poly, but it's **what you do with it** that counts.

But I'm only one little Square. How can **I make a difference**?

I have faith that you'll find a way. There is only one **"U"**, but figuring out how we can come **together** and become **"Us"** is where the magic happens.

Now motivated by
uncle Ken's tales of
travel around the world,
Poly began to walk back
with a growing excitement.

Poly's imagination was now filled with many new possibilities.

The next morning, Poly leapt out of bed and raced to the town square.

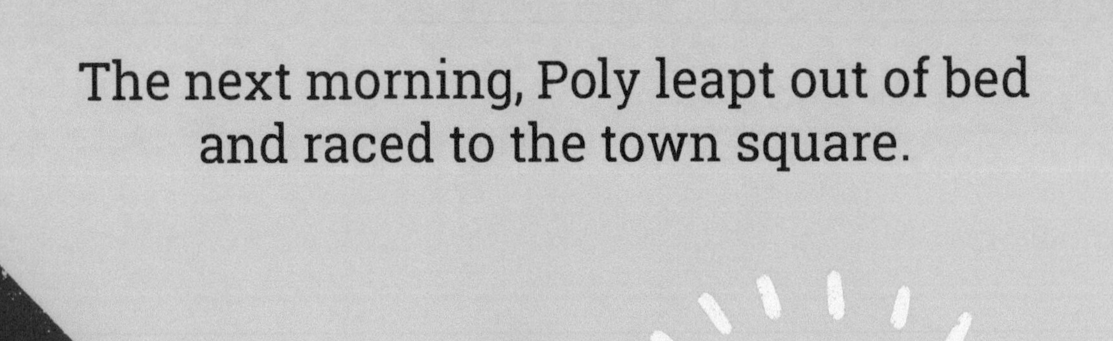

The shapes slowly slid,
rolled, flipped and
bounced over.

"Imagine what kind of town we could create if we all came **together**?" posed Poly.

"I don't understand," called out Octavius **Octagon**. "How will we all fit together?"

"Oh, if we put 5 triangles together, we can make a **Pentagon**," responded Trina **Triangle**.

"That's right!" exclaimed Poly.

"**2 triangles** could make a **square**, and **4** could make a **rectangle**," piped up Peter **Pentagon**.

"Yes, but let's think even **bigger**!" remarked Poly.

"If we **stack** a triangle on top of a square, we could start to make a sturdier **house**," chimed Hector **Heptagon**.

"Incredible ideas," beamed Poly. "If we all work together, we can create something beyond our imaginations."

The whole town got right to work, with everyone lending a hand.

She's always right.
She has acute angle.
Geometry 101

Blue Print
Under Construction

Mayor Hazel **Hexagon** slid over next to Poly to admire the new city.

Thanks! I am glad I was able to help.

We are individual 2-dimensional shapes, but by **working together**, we can be so much more! There's a space for everyone here now, whether you have sharp or curved edges, or whether all your sides are equal or not. I just had to think bigger...outside of myself...

outside of the square!

NEW 2D TOWN

Cast of Characters

Polygon Quadrilateral (a.k.a Poly)

I'm a **square.**

I have **4** equal, straight sides, and all my angles equal **90** degrees (they make an uppercase L shape).

Mrs. Quadrilateral (a.k.a Poly's mom)

I'm a **rhombus.**

All my **4** sides are straight, equal and my opposite sides are **parallel**.

Mr. Quadrilateral (a.k.a. Poly's dad)

I'm a **rectangle.**

I have **4** straight sides. My opposite sides are **equal** and all my angles are **90** degrees.

Auntie Quadrilateral

I'm a **trapezoid.**

I have **4** straight sides, with **1 pair** that are **parallel**.

Uncle Kenneth (a.k.a Ken)

I'm a **kite.** I have **4** sides.

My adjacent pairs of sides are equal.

Cara and Calvin

We are both **circles.**

We both have a **continuous curved line** that is called our circumference.

Major Hazel **Hexagon**

I have **6** equal, straight sides.

Octavius **Octagon**

I have **8** straight, equal sides.

Trina **Triangle**

I have **3** equal, straight sides.

Peter **Pentagon**

I have **5** equal, straight sides.

Hector **Heptagon**

I have **7** equal, straight sides.

Lightning Source UK Ltd.
Milton Keynes UK
UKHW051154180921
390774UK00002B/26